WHO is a SCIENTIST?

Laura Gehl

Ⓜ Millbrook Press / Minneapolis

Who is a scientist? This is a scientist.

ISHA is a meteorologist.

She studies the weather.

She also loves to dance, play volleyball, and eat chocolate.

Isha M. Renta López releases weather balloons and prepares weather forecasts. When there is a big weather event, such as a blizzard or a hurricane, she works with emergency response teams, the government, the media, and the public to make sure everyone knows what is happening and how to stay safe.

Who is a scientist? This is a scientist.

JAGMEET is a neuroscientist.

He studies how people and animals hear the sounds they make to communicate with one another. He also likes painting and taking photographs of birds, animals, and flowers.

Jagmeet Kanwal studies bats and zebrafish to help figure out how the human brain makes decisions. He wants to learn how our brains allow us to hear different types of sounds. One of Jagmeet's goals is to understand how music can help people with depression, Parkinson's disease, and memory loss.

Who is a scientist? This is a scientist.

MARINA is an engineer.

She studies rockets.

She also enjoys playing video games, practicing karate, and eating french fries.

Marina Gillett works for a company that makes rockets. She works on the avionics, which are the electronics that go in the rockets. Marina makes sure the engineering is done with the right tools, processes, and standards, so that the avionics are safe to go to space.

Who is a scientist? This is a scientist.

JONATHAN is an environmental scientist.

He studies food and culture.

He also loves cooking, sailing, and surfing.

Jonathan Fisk is studying Indigenous food systems and food sovereignty in Puerto Rico, where his family is from. Indigenous food systems are foods grown and eaten by the original people to live in a place. Food sovereignty is everyone's right to healthy and culturally appropriate food that is grown in ways that are good for the planet. It also means that people who produce food should have control over how it is grown and where it goes.

Who is a scientist? This is a scientist.

MUNAZZA is an astronomer.

She studies planets outside of our solar system.
She also likes to sketch, paint, and eat desserts.

Munazza Alam studies exoplanets, or planets outside of our solar system. She is particularly interested in the weather and atmospheres of those other planets. To figure out the weather forecast on faraway planets, Munazza uses data from the Hubble Space Telescope.

Who is a scientist? This is a scientist.

MARK is a mathematician.

He studies how math can be used to make people's lives better. He also enjoys playing basketball and watching movies.

EQN's

$(x,a) + \alpha \sum_{y \in X} k(y) P(y|x,a)$

DISCOUNTED COST
OPTIMALITY EQNS

Mark Lewis is a professor who focuses on operations research. Operations research uses math to help businesses make good decisions. Mark helps figure out how cars and trucks can get from place to place faster or how much items should cost when bought on the internet. Mark also studies waiting in lines and how to make the wait time shorter.

Who is a scientist? This is a scientist.

JOYCE is an agroecologist.

She studies natural ways to keep pest insects away from farms.
She also loves to swim, kayak, eat tacos, and wear lipstick.

Joyce Parker's work has helped farmers. She taught them how to grow "companion plants," plants that insects don't like, as a natural way to keep insects away from crops. Now Joyce works in the US government on programs that teach effective and sustainable ways to grow crops.

Who is a scientist? This is a scientist.

BOB is a neurobiologist.

He studies the brain.

He also likes to cook, read, and listen to music.

Sandeep Robert (Bob) Datta wants to understand how the brain gets information from the environment and then acts on that information. One of the ways Bob works to understand the brain is by studying how mice react to different smells, such as those from food, predators, and other mice.

Who is a scientist? This is a scientist.

JOLVAN is an environmental scientist.

She studies fish.

She also enjoys hiking, doing yoga, and riding her motorcycle, which she named Louisa.

Jolvan Morris studies real-life "dinosaurs" called Atlantic sturgeon. These prehistoric-looking fish are lined with bony plates, or scutes. The species has been around for 120 million years. Atlantic sturgeon can weigh up to 800 pounds (363 kg) and grow up to 14 feet (4.3 m) long. Because Atlantic sturgeon are protected by the Endangered Species Act, Jolvan gives students and teachers information about the act and how to "adopt" and track sturgeon to keep the species from going extinct.

Who is a scientist? This is a scientist.

NIZAR is a paleontologist.

He studies dinosaurs and other extinct animals.
He also loves dogs and playing soccer.

Nizar Ibrahim looks for fossils in remote places, such as the Sahara Desert in Africa. He has contributed to exciting discoveries including a new skeleton of *Spinosaurus*, a large predatory aquatic dinosaur.

Who is a scientist? This is a scientist.

MICHELLE is a mechanical engineer.

She works for the US Navy. She also likes to run, teach exercise classes, knit, and listen to live bands.

Michelle Skoorka works for the navy managing research and drone programs. She has studied corrosion (rust) in seawater. For fifteen years, she developed submarine launch systems.

Who is a scientist? This is a scientist.

TISHINA is a biomedical scientist.

She studies how to keep mothers and children healthy. She also enjoys visiting new places, belly dancing, and eating pizza and ice cream.

Tishina Okegbe travels to Africa and Asia to help with health-care projects. She works to make sure mothers, infants, and children have access to high-quality health-care services.

Who is a scientist? This is a scientist.

RICHARD is an entomologist.

He uses equipment like this to hear insects inside of trees.

He also loves to explore outside and spend time with family and friends.

Richard Mankin studies how to find and control groups of hidden insects. For example, insects might be hiding in a shipment of fruit coming to the United States from another country. Richard also studies how insects use smell and sound in communicating.

Who is a scientist? This is a scientist.

TARA is a software engineer.

She studies computers.

She also likes animals and playing sports.

Tara Astigarraga invents ways for businesses to keep track of information. She has invented more than seventy new types of computer programs and filed more than seventy patents.

A scientist is curious. A scientist asks questions.

A scientist searches for answers.

Some scientists work inside, in a lab or an office. Other scientists work outside, on a farm or in the desert.

Scientists can work in the ocean or in outer space.

Who is a scientist?
One day . . . maybe you!

Scan the QR code to meet the scientists!

qrs.lernerbooks.com/scientist

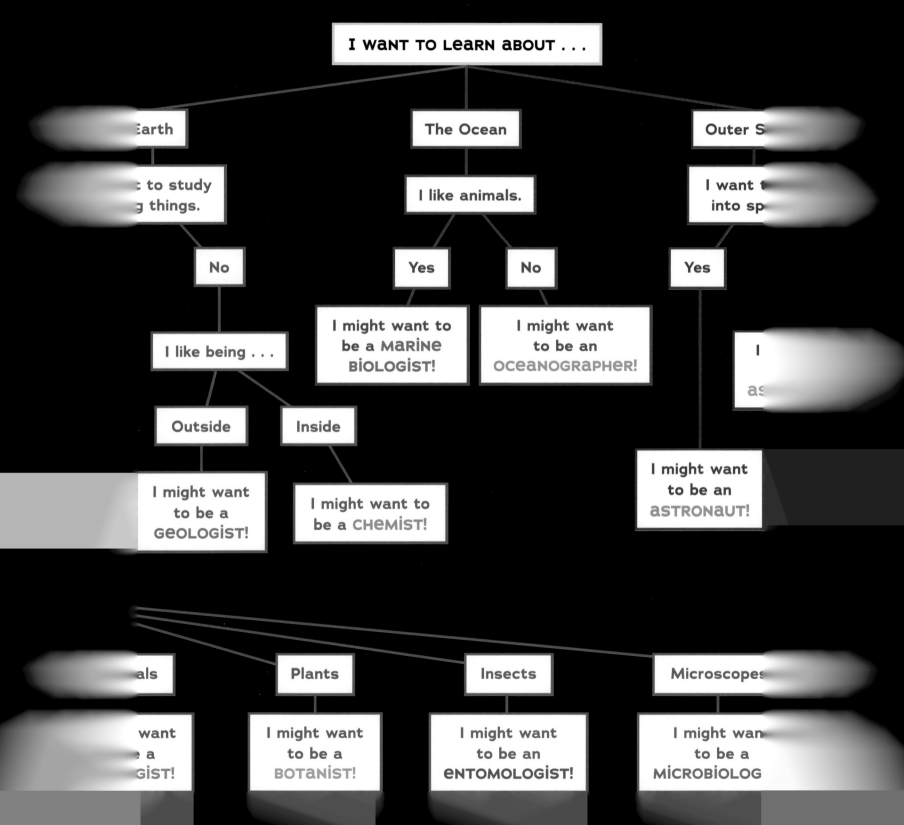

In memory of my dad, my first science teacher, whose hands-on lessons included ornithology, astronomy, chemistry, and microbiology. And for all of the scientists working today to advance human knowledge in countless different ways.

Millbrook Press™
An imprint of Lerner Publishing Group, Inc.
241 First Avenue North
Minneapolis, MN 55401 USA

For reading levels and more information, look up this title at www.lernerbooks.com.

Image credits: Ali Rae Haney Photography, pp. 2, 3, cover; Alexandra Taylor, pp. 4, 5, 22, 23, cover; Durjoy Siddique, pp. 6, 7, cover; Courtesy of Ohana Surf Project, pp. 8, cover; Justin Jansen, p. 9; Kristen Joy Emack, pp. 10, 11, cover; Robyn Wishna, pp. 12, 13, cover; Joyce Parker, p. 14; Conor Duffy, pp. 15, cover; Kristen Joy Emack, pp. 16, 17, 18, 19, cover; Athena Mishiyev, p. 20; Nanni Fontana, National Geographic Italy, pp. 21, cover; Tishina Okegbe, pp. 24, 25, cover; Richard Mankin, pp. 26, 27, cover; Lori Coleman, Lori & Erin Photography, pp. 28, 29, cover.

Designed by Viet Chu.
Main body text set in Adrianna. Typeface provided by Chank.

Library of Congress Cataloging-in-Publication Data

Names: Gehl, Laura, author.
Title: Who is a scientist? / Laura Gehl, PhD.
Description: Minneapolis, MN : Millbrook Press, [2022] | Audience: Ages 4–9 | Audience: Grades K–1 | Summary: "Scientists work hard in the lab and in the field to make important discoveries. But that's not all. They also love to dance, fly drones, eat french fries, and more! Meet fourteen phenomenal scientists" —Provided by publisher.
Identifiers: LCCN 2020030910 (print) | LCCN 2020030911 (ebook) | ISBN 9781541597990 (library binding) | ISBN 9781728419060 (ebook)
Subjects: LCSH: Scientists—Juvenile literature.
Classification: LCC Q147 .G44 2022 (print) | LCC Q147 (ebook) | DDC 509.2/2—dc23

LC record available at https://lccn.loc.gov/2020030910
LC ebook record available at https://lccn.loc.gov/2020030911

Manufactured in the United States of America
1-47991-48669-3/9/2021

Name Pronunciations

Laura Gehl: LOHR-rah GAYL

Isha Renta López: EE-shah REN-tah LOH-pez

Jagmeet Kanwal: JAG-meet CAN-wull

Marina Gillett: mah-REE-nah jihl-LEHT

Jonathan Fisk: JOHN-ah-thun FISK

Munazza Alam: moo-NUH-zah AHL-um

Mark Lewis: MAHRK LOO-iss

Joyce Parker: JOIS PAHR-ker

Sandeep (Bob) Datta: SAHN-deep BAWB DAT-tah

Jolvan Morris: JOHL-vahn MOR-iss

Nizar Ibrahim: NEE-zahr EEB-ruh-heem

Michelle Skoorka: mih-SHEL SKOR-kah

Tishina Okegbe: tih-SHEE-nah oh-KEE-bee

Richard Mankin: RICH-erd MAHN-kihn

Tara Astigarraga: TAIR-rah ah-STEE-gahr-RAH-gah